Understanding The Lay of the HOLY LAND

An Introductory Atlas

Yohanan Aharoni

cartaJerusalem

First published in 2019 by
CARTA Jerusalem

Partially excerpted from
The Carta Bible Atlas

11 Rivka Street, P.O.B. 2500,
Jerusalem 9102401, Israel
E-mail: carta@carta.co.il
www.carta-jerusalem.com

The scripture quotations are from the King James Version unless otherwise indicated.

Great care has been taken to establish sources of illustrations. If inadvertently we omitted to do so, due credit will be given in the next edition.

ISBN: 978-965-220-905-4

Printed in the United States of America

CONTENTS

THE FOUR WINDS OF THE HEAVENS AND THEIR NAMES

The Lord said to Abram ... Lift up now thine eyes, and look from the place where thou art northward, and southward, and eastward, and westward. For all the land which thou seest, to thee will I give it, and to thy seed for ever.

(Genesis 13:14–15)

To the north the winterbound, snow-covered mountains of the Lebanon; to the south the semiarid Negeb; to the east the wide desert; to the west the Great Sea — these are the natural borders of Canaan/Israel. Within their confines was enacted the history of Israel from the days of the Patriarchs on. A look at the landscape, its roads and ancient settlements, and the countries surrounding it are a prerequisite for a proper understanding of this history.

We possess no ancient map depicting the Holy Land in the biblical period. If such did exist, we can assume that it would face eastward, for in ancient Hebrew the word "forward" also means east, "behind" means west, "right" means south, and "left" means north. Benjamin ("the son of the right") is the southernmost of the Rachelite tribes; the Dead Sea is also referred to in Hebrew as the "forward (eastern) sea"; the Great Sea, the Mediterranean of today, is also called the "latter (western) sea."

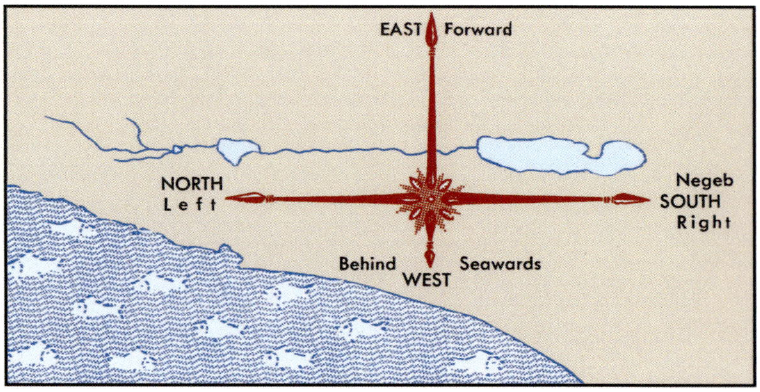

One of the oldest maps extant is the Medeba map. This is a mosaic floor dating from the sixth century A.D. in a church at Medeba, to the east of the Dead Sea. This map was intended to show the Holy Land of the Bible and faces eastward. At the center appears the Dead Sea, on which sail two boats. It was prepared more than one thousand years after the Destruction of the First Temple, and thus is of limited value for the identification of ancient sites.

(left) Section of the Medeba map in the Greek Orthodox Basilica of St. George (photo Jerzy Strzelecki, via Wikimedia Commons).

(below) Diagram of the Medeba map (place names translated from the Greek).

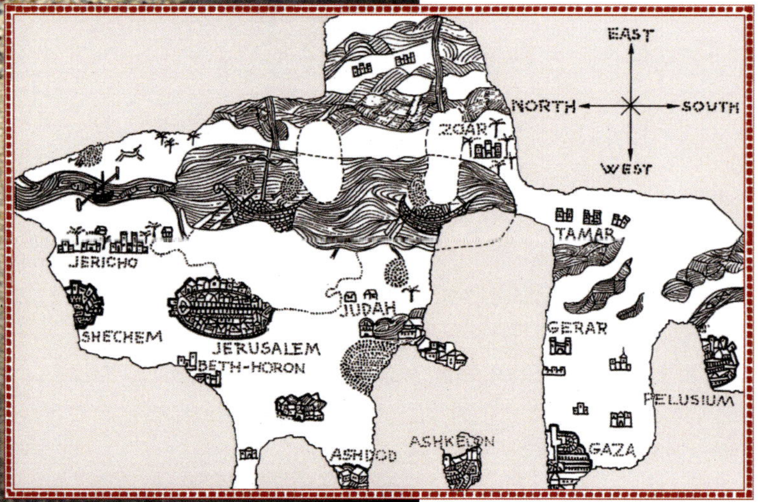

THE WAY TO SHILOH

Iron I remains at Shiloh (photo Samuel Magal).

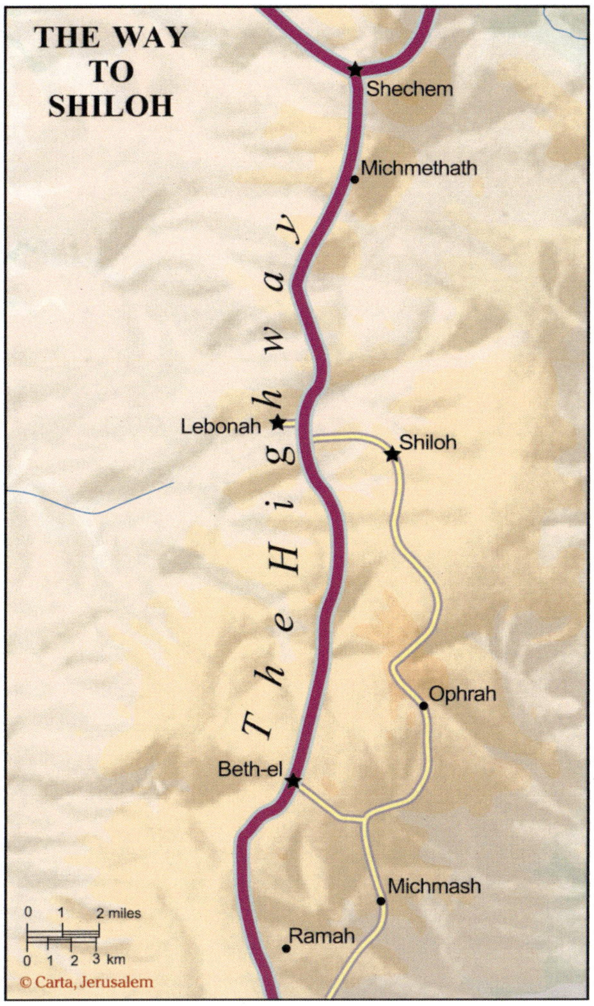

JUDG 21:19

I will send them, and they shall rise, and go through the land, and describe it according to the inheritance of them...

(Joshua 18:4)

The Bible does not, as a rule, give many descriptions of settlements, their location and character—these matters were taken for granted then. Only a few verses diverge from this rule, the outstanding case being the description of the site of Shiloh in the story of the abduction of wives for the Benjaminites: "Then they said, Behold, there is a feast of the Lord in Shiloh yearly in a place which is on the north side of Beth-el, on the east side of the highway that goeth up from Beth-el to Shechem, and on the south of Lebonah" (Judg 21:19). Nothing could be more accurate. Why did the biblical writer give such detail to the location of a site as famous in ancient times as Shiloh? Probably because Shiloh had been destroyed by the Philistines, and early in the period of the Monarchy, when the story was written down, it lay in ruins.

Unlike Shiloh, most locations are merely described in vague terms in the Bible. Thus, in reconstructing the ancient map of the Holy Land in the various periods, we must lean heavily on four factors:

1. Analysis of the history, character, and general topography of the individual site in the light of available sources;
2. Identifications in later sources;
3. The preservation of the ancient name, with possible modifications during transfer from Hebrew to Aramaic and Arabic; and
4. Archaeological examination of the site under consideration in the light of the above data.

THE ANCIENT NEAR EAST

Archaeological research has made great strides in our times, and many details of the map of the ancient Holy Land are now agreed upon.

The decisive geographical factor in the history of Canaan/Israel is its outermost position at the southwest end of the settled, fertile lands of the Near East. These lands stretch crescentlike from the Persian Gulf to the Sinai Peninsula: the so-called Fertile Crescent. On the west, this crescent touches the Mediterranean Sea. On the north and the east it is surrounded by high, nearly impassable mountains, the Amanus, Taurus, Ararat, and Zagros ranges. Within the hollow of the Fertile Crescent lies the extensive Syrian-Arabian Desert, extending on the west into the wilderness of Paran (the Sinai Peninsula). This latter separates the Holy Land from Egypt.

Today the Fertile Crescent is divided between Iraq, Syria, Lebanon, Jordan, and Israel; its fertility stems from two factors—flat lands and an abundance of water. This is especially true of the area known by the Greek name Mesopotamia—"between the two rivers." This is the richest part of the Fertile Crescent, whose broad plains are watered and fertilized by the flow of the two large rivers, the Tigris and the Euphrates. "The river" of the Bible is the Euphrates. Syria and Canaan/Israel are less fortunate, for they represent the narrow and lean parts of the Fertile Crescent and of the two Palestine is the smaller and the poorer; rivers are small and do not allow passage of boats; the riverbeds are deep and in ancient times there was little possibility of utilizing their waters for irrigation. Land is uneven and ridges leave only limited plains. Rains fall mostly in one season and their amount diminishes progressively as one goes farther south.

In spite of its being the smallest and the poorest section, at the edge of the Fertile Crescent, the land of Israel held an important geopolitical position as a bridge between the lands of the Fertile Crescent and Egypt, the land of the Nile. Mesopotamia on the one side, and Egypt on the other, were lands of large rivers, and in both of them the foundations of civilization were laid toward the end of the fourth millennium. Similar geographical and economic features assisted in the development of both these lands; there are extensive alluvial plains, whose fertility is dependent upon large, long rivers passing through them. A river is the primary integrating factor within each of the two countries. It provides convenient

From the wilderness and this Lebanon even unto the great river, the river Euphrates, all the land of the Hittites, and unto the great sea toward the going down of the sun, shall be your coast. (Joshua 1:4)

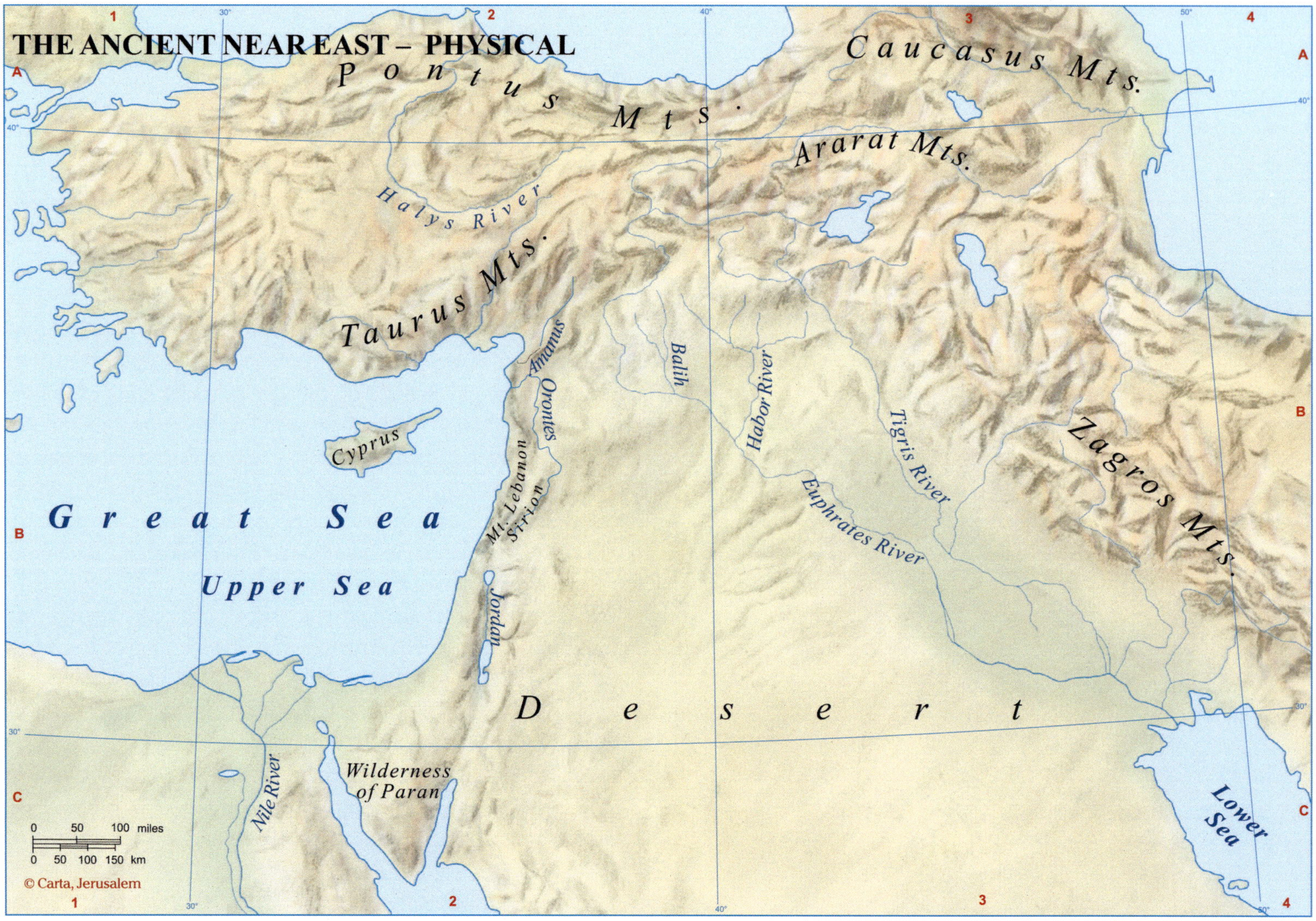

*(above) "**The** river" of the Bible, the Euphrates* (photo Zhengan, via Wikimedia Commons).

(below) Mount Ararat, from near the city of Artashat in Armenia (photo Serouj Ourishian, via Wikimedia Commons).

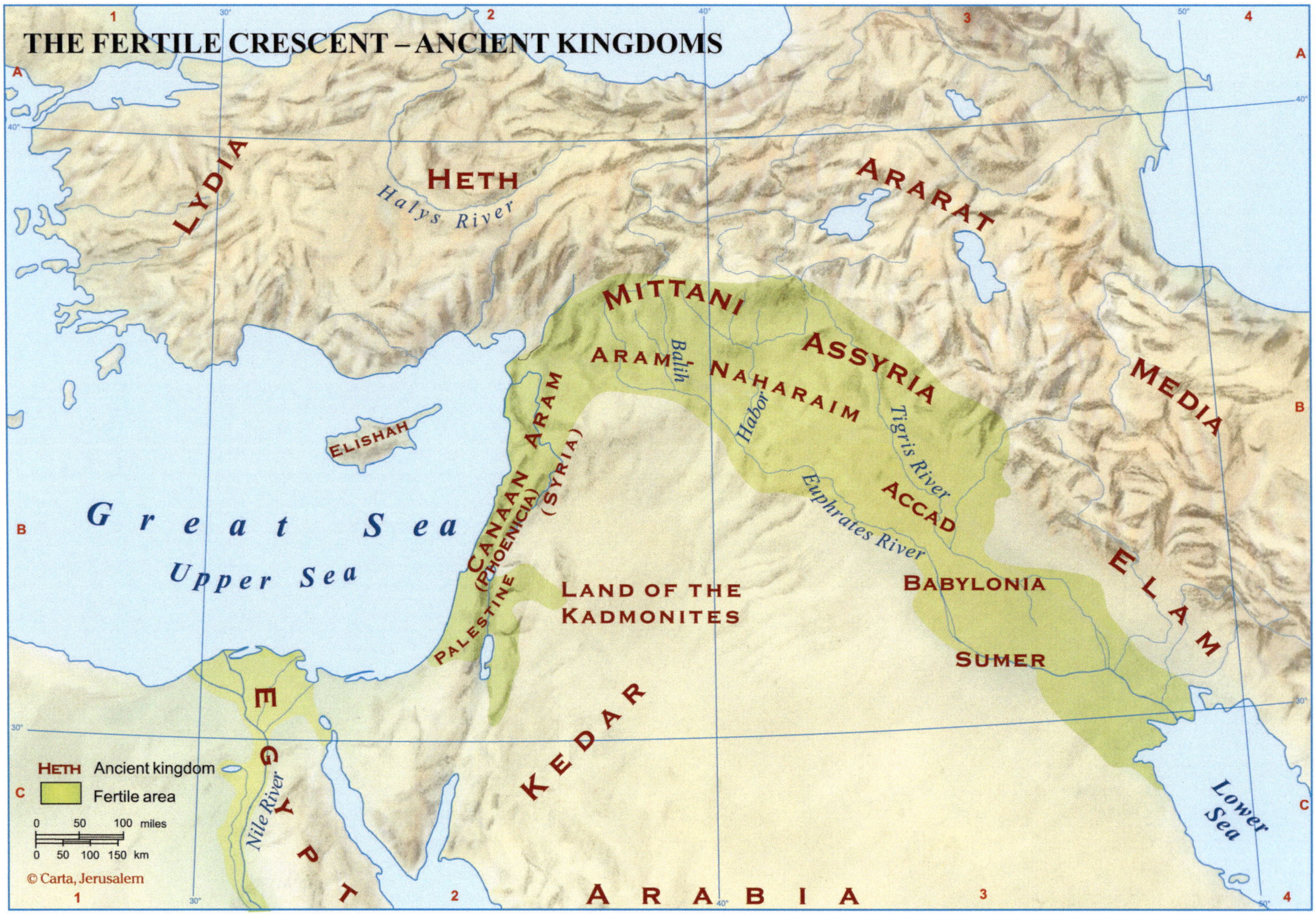

arteries of communication and irrigates the land. This, of course, was dependent upon there being a governmental apparatus capable of instilling order, peace, and security, and of mobilizing manpower for the construction of dams and canals on a wide scale. Under such conditions rose the first mighty kingdoms with the power to impose organization and unity on their individual settlements, and even rule over areas beyond their own borders. In the Fertile Crescent this was the historical stage on which appeared in succession Sumer and Accad, Mittani and the Hittites, and later the Arameans, the latter having given their name to the northern part of Mesopotamia — Aram-Naharaim. In contrast, Egypt was closely confined and homogeneous in development, only the various dynasties succeeding one another over the years, from the time of the Early Kingdom down through the Middle and into the Late Kingdoms. Communications between Egypt and the kingdoms of the Fertile Crescent passed of necessity through Canaan/Israel, thus establishing its destiny as a land-bridge. Military campaigns swept in succession through Canaan/Israel, which in many periods was held by one or the other of the great powers; yet no major cultural development came about in either civilization without Canaan/ Israel having some part in it.

Evening along the Nile (photo Rod Waddington, via Wikimedia Commons).

THE FERTILE CRESCENT – MODERN STATES
GREECE
GEORGIA
ARMENIA
AZERBAIJAN
Caspian Sea
TURKEY
Anatolian Plateau
KURDISTAN
IRAN (PERSIA)
Mesopotamia
SYRIA
CYPRUS
Mediterranean Sea
LEBANON
Syrian Desert
Tigris River
Euphrates River
IRAQ
ISRAEL
Jordan
JORDAN
EGYPT
International boundary
Fertile area
Sinai
Nafud Desert
KUWAIT
Persian Gulf
Western Desert
Nile River
0 50 100 miles
0 50 100 150 km
© Carta, Jerusalem
Red Sea
SAUDI ARABIA

THE DESERTS SURROUNDING CANAAN

And, behold, there came a geat wind from the wilderness...
(Job 1:19)

The Holy Land lies between the sea and the desert, and both influence its nature. The westerly wind brings life-giving rains, whereas the easterly brings only the dryness of the desert. The higher a place, or the closer to the sea, the more wet the climate.

The southern part of Canaan lies within an arid zone that runs around the globe; the extensive desert regions enclose the Holy Land on the south and east, with lofty Mount Seir jutting like a finger toward the heart of the wilderness.

There is no definitive natural border separating the settled area from the desert regions, and the hungry pastoralists of the steppe have beaten on the doors of the Holy Land since time immemorial. The influence of the steppe and the desert in the history of the Holy Land is profound and an awareness of this wilderness is echoed throughout the pages of the Bible.

Wilderness of Sinai (public domain, via Wikimedia Commons).

THE GEOGRAPHICAL REGIONS OF CANAAN

> In the mountains, and in the valleys, and in the plains, and in the springs, and in the wilderness...
>
> (Joshua 12:8)

The terrain of the Holy Land is quite varied, mainly because of sharp climatic differences from region to region. The major feature of the relief of the Holy Land and Syria is the deep rift stretching from northern Syria through the valley of Lebanon, the Jordan valley, the Arabah and the Gulf of Elath, down to the southeastern coast of Africa. This cleft divides Palestine into its western part and the eastern "Transjordan"; there are great differences in altitude within short distances. The distance between Hebron and the mountains of Moab as the crow flies is no more than 36 miles, though in traversing this, a descent from +3,000 feet down to –1,300 feet below sea level (the lowest spot on the face of the earth) is made, followed again by an ascent to more than 3,000 feet. These contrasts form the dry Arabah at the edge of the Judean Desert, with its rugged scarps, and opposite are the fertile and watered plateaus of Transjordan. These variations of land and climate brought about extremely different patterns of settlement within Palestine, which resulted in corresponding political divisions in most periods.

In several instances, the major distinct regions of the Holy Land are clearly defined and listed in the Bible according to topography and climate (Deut 1:7; Josh 10:40; 11:16; Judg 1:9; and so forth).

Even such a list as the geographical administrative classification of cities of Judah is divided into four major regions: the Negeb (south), the Shephelah (lowlands), the hill-country, and the wilderness (Josh 15:21, 33, 48, 61).

Negeb landscape (photo Samuel Magal).

THE GEOGRAPHICAL REGIONS OF CANAAN

View from Nahal David (near En-gedi) of the Dead Sea and Moab mountains (photo ekeidar, via Wikimedia Commons).

Snow-covered Mount Hermon (photo Samuel Magal).

The river Jordan (photo Samuel Magal).

... a land of hills and valleys, and drinketh water of the rain of heaven.

(Deuteronomy 11:11)

Panoramic view of the southern end of the Sea of Galilee, looking southeast (photo Zachi Evenor, via Wikimedia Commons).

The Arabah, looking east toward Mount Seir (photo Batya Ben Zvi, via Wikimedia Commons).

Galilee landscape (photo Samuel Magal).

THE INTERNATIONAL ROUTES IN THE ANCIENT EAST

The main highways played a most important part in the history of the Holy Land. The settlements of Palestine are located at the crossroads of the Ancient East. The most important route was the highway from Mesopotamia to Egypt, and on it were founded the important political centers. From earliest times commercial caravans plied the major highways, carrying their products, precious objects, and luxuries; and providing for the needs of the caravans, and their security, became a constant source of income. These ways, however, were not open for trade and commerce alone: military campaigns and conquests also trod them throughout history, leaving in their wake destruction and desolation. In most periods the Holy Land was dominated by major foreign powers, northern or southern, who mainly strove to secure a hold on these routes.

The mountainous nature of the Palestinian terrain dictates the courses of the roads. The principal international route connecting Egypt with North Syria and Mesopotamia traverses the southern Levant from south to north, following the line of the seacoast in the south until reaching the barrier of Nahal Kanah (Nahr el-'Auja) where it had to swerve eastward to go around Aphek.

It then skirted the eastern edge of the northern Sharon plain and passed to the Jezreel valley either via the valley of Aruna to Megiddo or via the valley of Dothan. From there it most probably went past Beth-shean, either north to Hazor and the Lebanese Beqa' or across the Jordan to Damascus. The segment from Egypt across Sinai was called "the Way of the god Horus" by the Egyptians and once it was called "way of the land of the Philistines" (Exod 13:17). Apart from that, this great international trunk route has no name either in the Bible or in extra-biblical sources, Roman or otherwise.

The second international route was the King's Highway (Num 21:22), which passes through the hill-country of Transjordan, close to the desert. This is the secondary route from Damascus to Egypt, its importance lying in the fact that the roads to Arabia branch off from it. There existed various other secondary, local roads, which were used largely by local traffic, and in time of need they also served as alternatives for international trade caravans. The maps show only the more important routes, especially those mentioned by name in the Bible.

We will go by the high way: and if I and my cattle drink of thy water, then I will pay for it...

(Numbers 20:19)

Ancient Mari, on the highway from Mesopotamia to Egypt. Shown here are the remains of a ziggurat near the palace (photo Heretiq, via Wikimedia Commons).

Coastal route along the Mediterranean, south of Rosh Haniqra near the Lebanese border (photo Takuya ASADA from Hachioji, Japan, via Wikimedia Commons).

Cast up, cast up the highway; gather out the stones...
(Isaiah 62:10)

The Crusader fortress of Kerak (biblical Kir-Moab), located on the King's Highway (photo Berthold Werner, via Wikimedia Commons).

Megiddo, a major crossroad in ancient times (photo Samuel Magal).

THE ECONOMY OF THE ANCIENT NEAR EAST

Food production was the basis of ancient economy. Diet was monotonous and much simpler than that of today; each area relied mainly upon its local produce. Although there were places where grain and other foodstuffs were marketed, the scope of such commerce was limited.

In the Ancient East grain production took place on the riverine plains. In the outlying, marginal regions, in the deserts and northern plains, sheep-raising was common, as was cattle and horse-breeding in certain areas. Camel-breeding on a large scale, mainly in the Arabian Desert, did not start until the end of the second millennium. The donkey was the chief beast of burden. In the Levant, too, grain was produced, though animal husbandry and horticulture were more important.

Another major branch of economy in the Ancient East was the smelting and working of metals. An important source of gold lay in the Land of Punt, to the south of Egypt; this may have been the biblical Ophir to which Solomon's ships sailed (1 Kgs 10:11, and so forth). The two most common metals, used in weapons and tools, were copper and iron, which were mainly produced in Asia Minor and the Caucasus, as well as in Cyprus. According to the Bible, iron and copper were mined in the mountains of the Holy Land (Deut 8:9); evidently reference is made here to the few mines in the marginal areas: the Valley of Lebanon, southern Gilead, and especially the copper mines on either side of the Arabah.

In the mountains of Lebanon and in the Anti-Lebanon (Sirion) stood forests of cedar and other woods, an important source of construction timber not only for Palestine and Syria, but also for Egypt and Mesopotamia. The forests of the Hauran and Mount Seir (Edom) probably served only local needs.

The coastal cities became centers of the textile industry, partly because they were close to the source of the Murex shells used in making "Tyrian purple," a dye reserved for precious textiles. The Hellenistic name for Canaan, Phoenicia, is connected with the Greek word for reddish-purple — *phoenix*. In documents of the fourteenth century B.C. found at Ugarit—the port city on the north Syrian coast—mention is made of textiles imported from Acco, Ashdod,

He that tilleth his land shall be satisfied with bread...
(Proberbs 12:11)

Caravan of Asiatics, tomb wall painting at Beni Hassan, 1890 B.C. (Carta collection).

and Ashkelon. In both Ugaritic documents and later Accadian sources, Ashdod and possibly also Ashkelon are mentioned as centers of fish exports. Thus, we may assume that a fish-preserving industry existed in the southern coastal cities. It seems that in various periods salt was obtained from the Dead Sea and from Mount Sodom, as witnessed by the name "Ir-hammelah"— the city of salt—at the northwestern end of the Dead Sea. The cultivation of various types of aromatic gums for perfumes in the Dead Sea region was also of some importance, the region having the proper climate for such. The main centers of perfume production, however, lay in southern Arabia.

The various crafts remained the trade secrets of family and tribal associations within particular areas. A speciality in the Jordan Valley, near Succoth, was the casting of metal utensils (1 Kgs 7:46), as confirmed by archaeological excavations at Succoth proper. At Tell Beit Mirsim (Ashan), on the border of the Shephelah, a quarter originally settled by textile dyers was uncovered.

A well-developed art in Canaan was ivory carving, the luxury product being used by the wealthy and royalty in architectural and furniture ornamentation. Tusks were imported from Cush (Nubia) and the land of Ni'i in northern Syria. The centers of this industry in the Canaanite period were located along the coast and. in the Israelite period, primarily at Damascus, Hamath, and perhaps Samaria.

Commerce thus generally occupied an important position in the economy of the southern Levant, especially in those areas along the main trade routes.

Egyptian merchant ship from the days of Hatshepsut, c. 1500 B.C. (Carta collection).

THE ECONOMY OF CANAAN / ISRAEL
Great Sea
Byblos
Cun
Berothah
Sidon
Damascus
Tyre
Hazor
Acco
Ashtaroth
Kenath
Dor
Megiddo
Ramoth-gilead
Shechem
Joppa
Rabbath-bene-ammon
Jericho
Jerusalem
Ashdod
City of Salt
Ashkelon
Gaza
Ashan
En-gedi
Zoar
Tamar
Punon
Elath
Copper
Salt
Iron
Metalwork
Sheep
Camels
Horses
Caravans
Carttle
Wheat
Barley
Textiles
Tyrian purple
Perfume
Cedars
Sycamores
Fishing
Dates
Forests
Construction timber
Fruit trees
0 10 20 miles
0 10 20 30 km
© Carta, Jerusalem

A land of wheat, and barley, and vines, and fig trees, and pomegranates; a land of oil olive, and honey ... a land whose stones are iron, and out of whose hills thou mayest dig brass.
(Deuteronomy 8:8–9)

(above) Two shells of Bolinus brandaris, *the spiny dye-murex, a source of the Tyrian purple dye* (photo M. Violante, via Wikimedia Commons).

Palm trees near the Dead Sea (photo Samuel Magal).

(below) Grazing sheep in Israel (photo Davidbena, via Wikimedia Commons).

THE EARLY CULTURES IN THE MIDDLE EAST

The first blossoms of human civilization are recognized in the development of food production (agriculture) and in the founding of towns and organized settlements. Traces of such are found already in the Middle Stone Age (Mesolithic), some 10,000 years ago. According to our present knowledge, Jericho is the oldest city in the world, for in the seventh millennium it was already surrounded by a massive stone wall. Jarmo, in northern Mesopotamia, is more or less contemporary, though it appears to have been no more than a village. Only future research will prove whether Jericho was truly the first city and unique at that time, and whether to the Jordan Valley, the smallest of the river valleys of the Fertile Crescent, belongs the designation "the cradle of civilization."

During the fifth millennium (the Late Stone Age—Neolithic), and the fourth millennium (the Chalcolithic), the progress of man is in evidence throughout the Fertile Crescent. In this period, Mesopotamia takes to the fore, but in Egypt, too, parallel developments are taking place, as also in the countries between—Palestine and Syria. These early cultures are today named after the sites where they were first discovered; in the comparative table the major cultures are listed chronologically.

Comparative Chronology of Early Civilizations

Period	*Date*	*Mesopotamia*	*Syria-Palestine*	*Egypt*
Neolithic (Late Stone Age)	5000 4000	Jarmo Hassuna, Nineveh I Samarra Nineveh II	Jericho IX Byblos A Ras Shamra V (Ugarit) Amuq	El-Fayum A
Chalcolithic (Stone-Copper Age)	4000 3500	Tell Halaf	Megiddo XX Hamath L Yarmuk (Shaar Ha-Golan) Jericho VIII	Deir Tasa El-Badari
	3500 3150	Tell el-Ubeid Erech	Teleilat Ghassul, Beer-sheba	El-Amrah Nagada I
Early Bronze Age I	3150 2850	Jemdet Nasr	Early Canaanite Period I	El-Gerzeh, Nagada II

... where thou sowedst thy seed, and wateredst it with thy foot, as a garden of herbs.

(Deuteronomy 11:10)

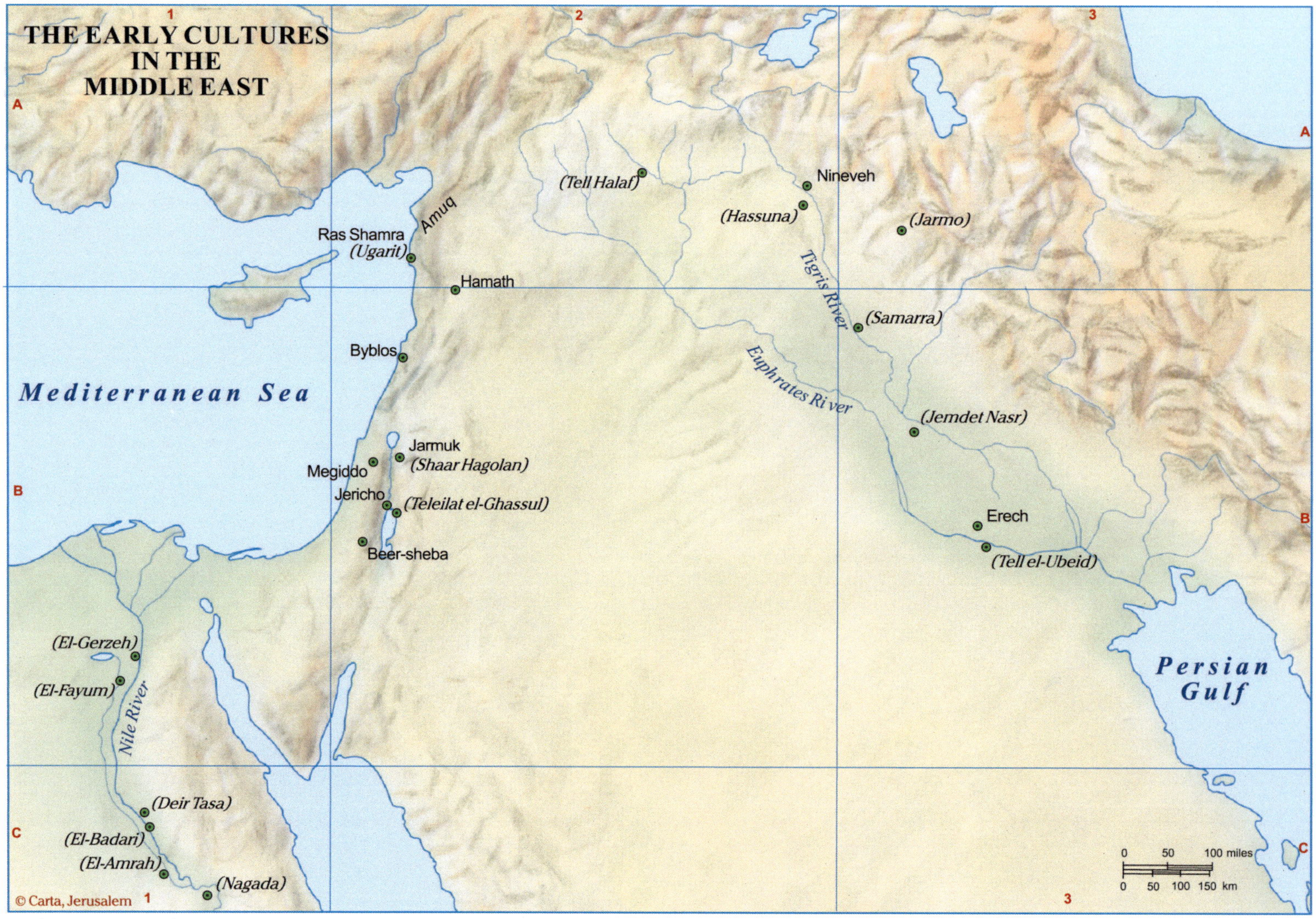

Ancient Jericho (Tell es-Sultan) (photo Berthold Werner, via Wikimedia Commons).

THE RIVERS OF THE GARDEN OF EDEN

GEN 2:10–14

And a river went out of Eden to water the garden; and from thence it was parted, and became into four heads.

(Genesis 2:10)

Where are the ancient centers of civilization according to the Bible? The answer to this is hinted at in the description of the four rivers emerging from the Garden of Eden. It is natural that the ancients should believe the rivers of Eden to be those flowing through the lands most abundant in water, the foremost being the Tigris and the Euphrates in Mesopotamia. The Pishon and the Gihon have not been identified and may have merely been symbolic. But since Havilah is one of the regions of Cush (Gen 10:7), it would seem that the two major branches of the Nile (the Blue and the White) may have been intended.

(below) Blue Nile near Bahar Dar, Ethiopia (photo Giustino, via Wikimedia Commons)..

THE FAMILIES OF THE NATIONS IN THEIR LANDS (TABLE OF NATIONS)

In the Bible there has been preserved a unique list of the nations of the world, within the scope of the people of Israel, the list of the family of man ("the generations of the sons of Noah"). The lands of the world and the peoples are divided into three main lines: the sons of Shem in Mesopotamia and Arabia, the sons of Ham in Egypt and within its sphere of influence, and the sons of Japheth in the northern and western lands. Included in the list are also royal cities and important centers within the Fertile Crescent: in the land of Shinar (southern Mesopotamia) and the land of Canaan. Even if not all the identifications are certain—and some of the names have not been identified at all—the general division is quite clear: three spheres of peoples and lands, which meet in the region of the Holy Land.

By these were the isles of the Gentiles divided in their lands; every one after his tongue, after their families, in their nations.
(Genesis 10:5)

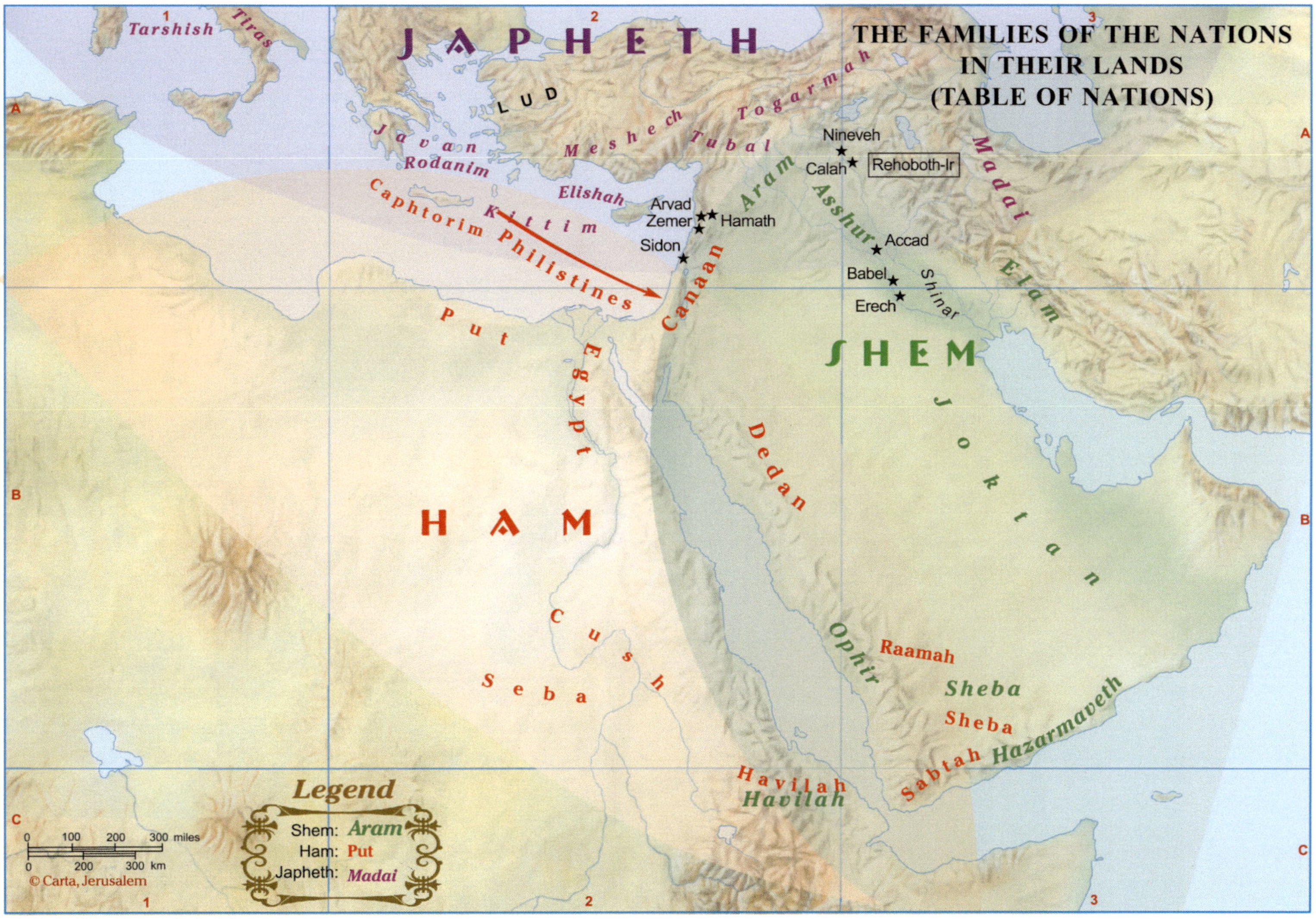

GEN 10; 1 CHR 1:4–23

Ham—Teye, Queen of Egypt (beginning of 14th century B.C.)

Japheth — (Cretan wall painting at Knossus)

Shem—Assyrian (relief from palace af Sargon at Khorsabad)

ARCHAEOLOGICAL EXCAVATIONS IN THE HOLY LAND

Biblical geography in a serious sense began about one hundred and eighty years ago with the survey trip of Edward Robinson in 1838. He recorded many biblical place names still preserved in Arabic dress. However, he and many who came after him did not recognize that the village bearing a biblical name might not be on the original spot of the Old Testament site. In 1891, Frederick J. Bliss proved what others had been claiming for some time, namely that the prominent, flat-topped mounds located at strategic points around the country were actually the accumulation of debris from city upon city, built up during the ages. Such a mound is usually called a tell, a Semitic term signifying "mound" or "hillock," which gradually acquired the specific usage as a designation of a mound made up of ancient debris. Archaeological surveys since Robinson not only recorded Arabic place names, they also mapped the country and indicated the ecological and sociological details of the terrain and of the population. Flinders Petrie's excavation at Tell el-Hesi inaugurated the activity of excavation in Palestine following the example of giants like A. H. Layard in Assyria and H. Schliemann at

Edward Robinson (1794–1863) (photo public domain, Nordisk Familjebok).

The remains of Robinson's Arch,named after the archaeologist who discovered it. Located at the southwestern corner of the Temple Mount; it once supported a staircase which led to the temple in Jerusalem (photo Samuel Magal).

Frederick J. Bliss, c. 1894–1897 (photo public domain, courtesy Palestine Exploration Fund).

Sir Austen Henry Layard (by John Sartain after H. W. Philips, public domain, via Wikimedia Commons).

Heinrich Schliemann as a young man (Uniphoto Press, via Wikimedia Commons).

Sir (William Matthew) Flinders Petrie (by Ludwig Blum, painted in Jerusalem in 1937; public domain, courtesy of Mira Chen, Ludwig Bloom's granddaughter).

Tell el-Hesi, first excavated by Flinders Petrie in 1890 (photo Guy Gotlib, via Wikimedia Commons).

Troy. It became clear that these tells were built up from the successive construction and destruction of settlements on the same site. As a city was destroyed, buildings disintegrated, adding yet another layer of rubble to the height of the tell. During the Bronze and Iron Ages, these sites tended to remain at locations with favorable conditions for sustaining human habitation, namely good water, arable land, defensible positions and routes of communication.

The Arabic form of *tell* is spelled "tell" in English, whence the English loan word; the modern Hebrew form is spelled "tel." The past ninety years have seen numerous large-scale excavations at such major sites. Techniques of recording and analyzing the finds are continually becoming more refined. The layers of debris are the main focus of the excavation; occupation layers are called *strata* (hence: stratigraphy). All the architectural features and other artifacts are ascribed to their respective layers. The meticulous differentiation of strata is based on the physical relationship of the features to one another; the relative dating is based on the nature of the artifacts found in each stratum, especially stone tools and pottery vessels (usually in fragments). Pottery is ideally suited to this task for two reasons: when a vessel is broken it becomes worthless and is discarded; but the ceramic fragments, especially of vessels fired in a kiln, are as hard as stone and thus survive the ravages of time (unlike organic materials which soon disintegrate in the moist soil). The abundance of potsherds in each layer are classified according to their style and type (thus: typology). The progressive development of local pottery styles and the appearance of imported styles from neighboring cultures are becoming more and more recognizable as the volume of excavated (and published) material increases. Comparison of the finds in the various strata of different excavations is gradually building up an acknowledged scale of ceramic typology for archaeological dating. The discovery of inscriptions or imported objects of datable artistic styles also helps to refine the dating.

For the historical periods, it may also be possible to compare the successive strata and occasional destruction layers with the recorded historical events pertaining to a particular site, or more often to the general region in which a site is located. However, such comparisons are a tricky business and great caution must be exercised; too often, scholars have jumped to premature conclusions about the supposed "historical" dating of this or that excavated stratum. Many new laboratory procedures, are advancing our knowledge.

As a proper background for excavations, the archaeological survey seeks to gather all the relevant data available for reconstructing the means of subsistence, the pattern of site locations and so forth. The goal is to achieve a picture of human habitation in all its facets in a particular physical setting.

The earliest cultures in the history of the Holy Land are known to us only from archaeological research. Discoveries in the Jordan Valley have proven that man appeared in Palestine in the Lower Pleistocene Age, estimated to be at least half a million years ago. This early man lived in the Levant before the final depression of the Jordan Valley to its present depth. In several caves in Mount Carmel and in Galilee, skeletons of Paleolithic man have been uncovered. These are of the more advanced type of Neanderthal man discovered in Europe. The scientific name of this type is *Palaeanthropus Palaestinensis*—"Early Palestinian Man." The last phase of the cave dwellers, in the Mesolithic Age (about 10,000 to 8000 B.C.), parallels the end of the last Ice Age in Europe. At this time began the first true settlement in the Levant; no major climatic changes have taken place since then. The earliest culture has been termed Natufian, after caves in Wadi en-Natuf on the western slopes of the central hill-country. This was a transitional phase of man, from hunting and gathering of food to crude agriculture and animal husbandry.

The revolutionary transition of man in the Levant, from cave dweller to founder of villages and towns, is best seen at Jericho, the one city of this period known to show such extensive accomplishments in construction and technology. This is in contrast to the usual open sites scattered here and there near readily arable land.

The progress of early civilizations was not always smooth

THE CHALCOLITHIC PERIOD
4TH MILLENNIUM B.C.
Dan
Beisamun
Yiron
Achzib
Nahal Dishon
Bet Ha'Emek
Hazor
Katzrin
Rasm Harbush
Acco
'Ain el-Hariri
Tel Chinnereth
Tell Keisan
Shiqmona
Tell Abu Hawam
'Enot Zippori
'Enot Sho'im
Naveh Yam
Etzba' Cave
Tell 'Ali
Tel Nami
'Ain Jerba
Tel Qiri
Tel Kishiyon
Dor
Tell Abu Zariq
'Afula
Munhata
Khirbet Sitt Leila
Megiddo
Naveh Or
Tel Mevorakh
Tel Kedesh
Tel Esur
Taanach
Beth-shean
Metzer
Rehob
Hadera
Tel Hefer
Tel Zeror
Tel Zaf
Pella
Ma'abarot
Dothan
Tell el-Far'ah North (Tirzah)
Tell es-Sa'idiyeh
Shechem
River Jordan
Tel Michal
Tell Deir 'Allah
Tel Gerisa
Wadi Rabba
Aphek
Tell el-Umeiri
Azor
Pezael
Nahal Shiloh
Lod
Yavneh-yam
Ben Shemen
Beth-el
Wadi 'Auja
Rabbath-ammon
Palmahim
Naveh Jericho
Jericho
Gezer
Tel Mor
Gibeon
Tel Miqne (Ekron)
Teleilat el-Ghassul
Ashdod
Tel Batash
Jerusalem
Beth-shemesh
Judean Desert Caves
Tel Zafit
Ashkelon
Be'er Adullam
Tell Judeideh
Beth-zur
Tell el-Hesi
Lachish
Hebron
Tell el-'Ajjul
En-gedi
Tell Beit Mirsim
Deir el-Balah
Cave of the Treasure
Tell Jemmeh
Tel Sera'
Khirbet Rabud
Nahal Gerar
Tel Haror
Nahal Mishmar
Gilat
Tel Halif
Nahal Besor
Tell el Far'ah (South)
Arad (Tel Arad)
Be'er Ze'elim
Be'er Osnat
Shiqmim
Tel Esdar
Site with Chalcolithic remains
0 5 10 miles
0 10 20 km.
© Carta, Jerusalem
A
B
C
D
E
1
2
3

Valley of the Caves (Wadi el-Mughara), sites of human evolution at Mount Carmel (photo Yitzhak Marmelstein, via Wikimedia Commons).

Reconstruction of a Natufian burial at el-Wad, in the Valley of the Caves (photo האיל הניאוליתי, via Wikimedia Commons).

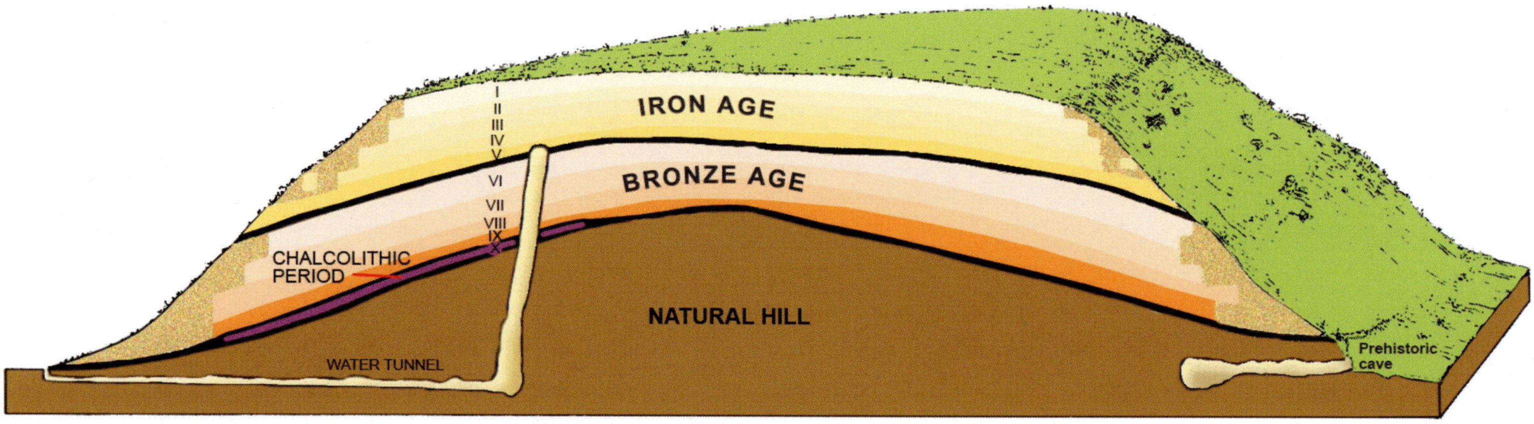

Schematic section of a tell (Carta collection).

and peaceful. Declines and retrogressions followed peaks of achievement. New conquering people dislodged inhabitants from their settlements, or settled in their midst. In the Chalcolithic period (the fourth millennium B.C.) many settlements were founded, mainly in the fertile valleys and on the edge of the desert. It was at this time that copper first came into use alongside stone implements. The later phase of this age is called the Ghassulian culture, after a group of small mounds in the southeastern part of the Jordan Valley, where the culture was first discovered (Teleilat el-Ghassul); it later became well known from several sites near Beer-sheba. These settlements spread over wide areas and were not fortified; the inhabitants were engaged in agriculture, herding, and household industries, including copper working. Their technical and artistic achievements are quite remarkable. A cache of copper utensils found in the "Cave of the Treasure" in the Judean Desert surpasses in both quality and beauty all other such objects known from the East from the same period. Among the lands of the early civilizations, Palestine held a respectable position till the end of the fourth millennium B.C.

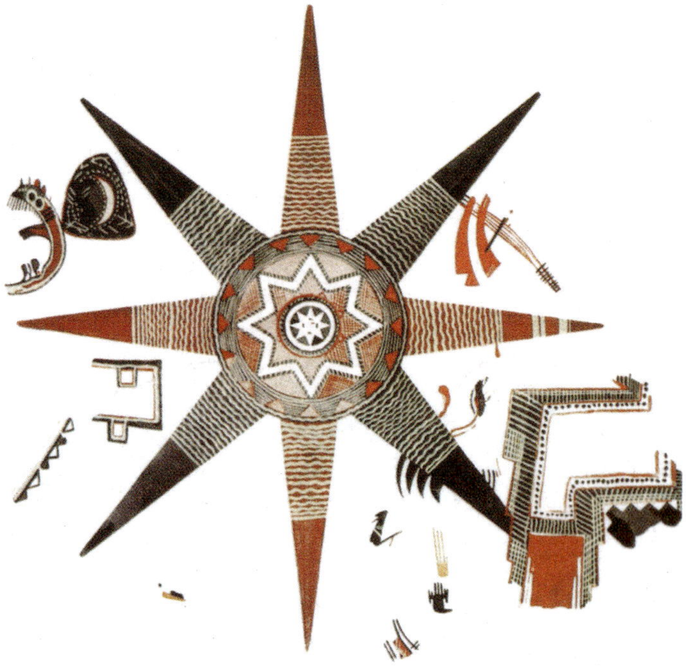

Chalcolithic wall painting from Teleilat el-Ghassul (IES).

Middle Bronze Age (Canaanite) remains of the high place at Tel Gezer (photo Samuel Magal).

THE BRONZE AGE
3150 TO 1200 B.C.
Ha-Gosherim
Dan
Kedesh
'Enan
Rosh Haniqra
Achzib
Hazor
Kabri
Meiron
Nahariya
Tel Harashim
Tel Bira
Tel Acco
Tel Chinnereth
Tell Keisan
Tel Raqqat
Tell Abu Hawam
Tel Regev
Beth-yerah
Athlit
Tel Qashish
Hazorea
Tell Kision
Sha'ar Hagolan
Tel Nami
Dor
Jokneam
'Afula
Tel Kitan
Megiddo
Tel Kedesh
Tel Mevorakh
Taanach
Beth-shean
El-Husn
Pehel
(Pella)
Tel Esur
Metzer
Rehob
Tel Zeror
Dothan
Tell el-Hayyat
Tel Hefer
Tirzah
Yaqum
Zaphon
Poleg
Succoth
Shechem
Tel Michal
River Jordan
Tel Gerisa
Aphek
Tell Umm Hammad
Joppa
Shiloh
'Ein Samiya
Beth-el
Rabbath-bene-ammon
Yavneh-yam
Ai
Gezer
Tell en-Nasbeh
Tel Mor
Jericho
Iktanu
Ashdod
Gibeon
Timnah
Jerusalem
Tel Miqne
(Ekron)
Beth-shemesh
Tel Jarmuth
Ashkelon
Tell es-Safi
Azekah
Tel Zippor
Beth-zur
Lachish
Tel 'Erani
Hebron
Tell el-Hesi
Khirbet Iskander
Gaza
Tel Nagila
Jebel Qa'aqir
Aroer
Tell el-'Ajjul
Tell Beit Mirsim
Tell Jemmeh
Khirbet Rabud
Balua
Tel Sera'
Sheikh ez-Zuweid
Arad
Tell el-Far'ah
(South)
Bab edh-Dhra
Tel Masos
Tel Malhata
Ader
Mashabei Sadeh
Mount Yeroham
Sites with Bronze Age remains
0 5 10 miles
0 10 20 km.
© Carta, Jerusalem
Be'er Resisim
1 2 3
A B C D E

THE IRON AGE
1200 TO 587 B.C.
Dan
Kedesh
Achzib
Hazor
Tel Harashim
Acco
Tel Bira
Tel Hadar
Chinnereth
Karnaim
Shiqmona
Tell Keisan
Tell Abu Hawam
Tel Regev
En-gev
Tell el-Wawiyat
Tel Megadim
Tell el-'Amr
Dor
Jokneam
'Afula
Megiddo
Jezreel
Tel Mevorakh
Taanach
Beth-shean
Ramoth-gilead
Tel Zeror
Tel 'Amal
Rehob
Pehel
Dothan
River Jordan
Tel Hefer
Tell el-Far'ah North
Tell es-Sa'idiyeh
Samaria
Tirzah
Shechem
Zaphon
Tell Mazar
Makmish
Tell Deir 'Allah (Succoth)
Mezad Hayarqon
Tell Qasile
'Izbet Sartah
'Ain Ghazal
Shiloh
Joppa
Tel Gerisa
Kh. Marjameh
Rabbath-bene-ammon
Beth-el
Mezad Hashavyahu
Ai
Tell en-Nasbeh
Jericho
Gezer
Tel Mor
Tel Batash (Timnah)
Gibeon
Gibeah of Saul
Jerusalem
Khirbet Qumran
Heshbon
Ashdod
Ekron
Beth-shemesh
Ramat Rahel
Mount Nebo
Ashkelon
Tell es-Safi
Tel Jarmuth
Azekah
Tel Zippor
Tell el-Judeideh
Tel 'Erani
Bozrah
Lachish
Mareshah
Beth-zur
Gaza
Tell el-Hesi
Tel Nagila
Hebron
Dibon
Tell Eitan
Aroer
En-gedi
Ruqeish
Deir el-Balah
Tell Beit Mirsim
Tel Haror
Tel Sera'
Balua
Tell Jemmeh
Tel Halif
Tell el-Far'ah South
Sheikh ez-Zuweid
Arad
Tel 'Ira
Horbat 'Uza
Beer-sheba
Tel Masos
Tel Malhata
Tell Esdar
Aroer
Mezad Gozal
Mezad Tamar
Horbat Ritma
Ha-Ro'a Site
Ramat Matred
Mezad Hazeva
Khirbet en-Nahas
Kadesh-barnea
Umm el-Biyara
Tawilan
Horbat Teman
Sites with Iron Age remains
0 5 10 miles
0 10 20 km.
© Carta, Jerusalem
Tell el-Kheleifeh
Ezion-geber
1
2
3
4
A
B
C
D
E

Iron Age (Israelite) remains at Tel Dan (photo Samuel Magal).

(above) Remains of a Hellenistic tower at Samaria (photo Samuel Magal).

(left) Relief of Nike, goddess of victory, standing on the heavenly globe supported by Atlas; part of the Severan forum's decoration at Ashkelon, 3rd century A.D. (photo Samuel Magal).

INDEX TO PLACES

T

U

V

W

Y

Z